956
Jo
Jordan in pictures

JORDAN

...in Pictures

Independent Picture Service

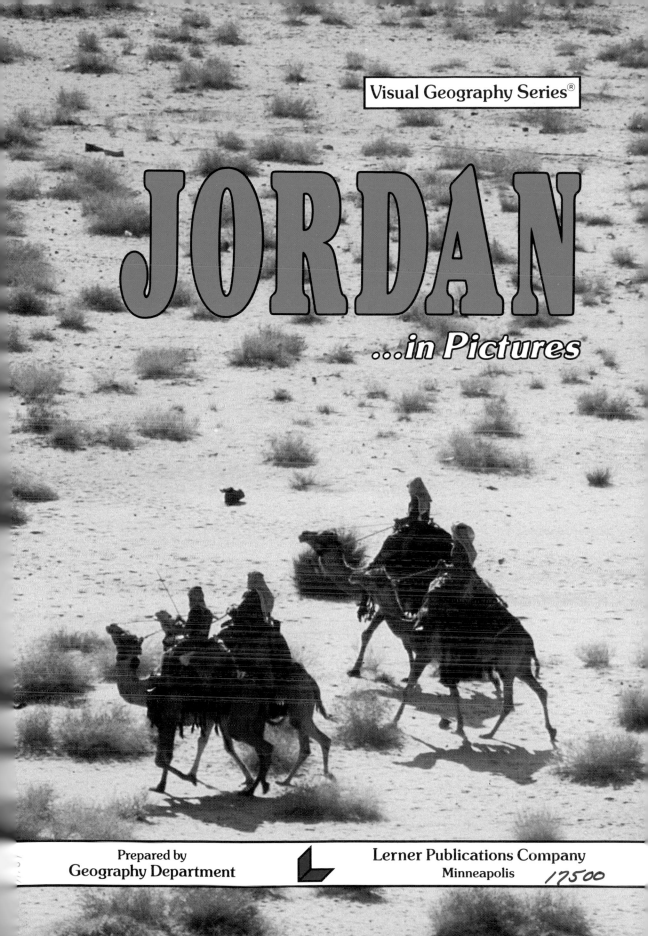

Visual Geography Series®

JORDAN

...in Pictures

Prepared by
Geography Department

Lerner Publications Company
Minneapolis

17500

Courtesy of UNRWA

**In the refugee camp at Aqabat Jaber, a Palestinian woman
makes one of her daily trips to a spring for water.**

This is an all-new edition of the Visual Geography
Series. Previous editions have been published by Ster-
ling Publishing Company, New York City, and some
of the original textual information has been retained.
New photographs, maps, charts, captions, and updated
information have been added. The text has been en-
tirely reset in 10/12 Century Textbook.

LIBRARY OF CONGRESS CATALOGING-IN-PUBLICATION DATA

Jordan in pictures / prepared by Geography Department,
Lerner Publications Company.

  p. cm. — (Visual geography series)
  Rev. ed. of: Jordan in pictures / by Camille Mirepoix
Stegmuller.
  Includes index.
  Summary: Text and photographs introduce the
geography, history, government, people, and economy
of Jordan.
  ISBN 0-8225-1834-1 (lib. bdg.)
  1. Jordan. [1. Jordan.] I. Mirepoix, Camille. Jordan
in pictures. II. Lerner Publications Company. Geog-
raphy Dept. III. Series: Visual geography series
(Minneapolis, Minn.)
DS 153.J68 1988   87-26455
956.95'04—dc19   CIP
                                               AC

International Standard Book Number: 0-8225-1834-1
Library of Congress Catalog Card Number: 87-26455

VISUAL GEOGRAPHY SERIES®

Publisher
Harry Jonas Lerner
Associate Publisher
Nancy M. Campbell
Senior Editor
Mary M. Rodgers
Editor
Gretchen Bratvold
Assistant Editors
Dan Filbin
Kathleen S. Heidel
Illustrations Editor
Karen A. Sirvaitis
Consultants/Contributors
Dr. Ruth F. Hale
Isaac Eshel
Sandra K. Davis
Designer
Jim Simondet
Cartographer
Carol F. Barrett
Indexer
Sylvia Timian
Production Manager
Gary J. Hansen

Courtesy of Jordan Information Bureau, Washington, D.C.

**Two men play mancala—one of the oldest and most wide-
ly played games in the world.**

Acknowledgments

Title page photo courtesy of Tor Eigeland/*Aramco
World*.

Elevation contours adapted from *The Times Atlas of
the World*, seventh comprehensive edition (New York:
Times Books, 1985).

2 3 4 5 6 7 8 9 10 97 96 95 94 93 92 91 90 89

Independent Picture Service

Built by the Umayyads in the eighth century A.D., Qasr (castle) al-Kharana served as a fortress and hunting lodge southeast of Amman. Inside, the grimness of its heavy stone walls is relieved by the carvings and frescoes (paintings on plaster) in the walls of the upper chamber.

Contents

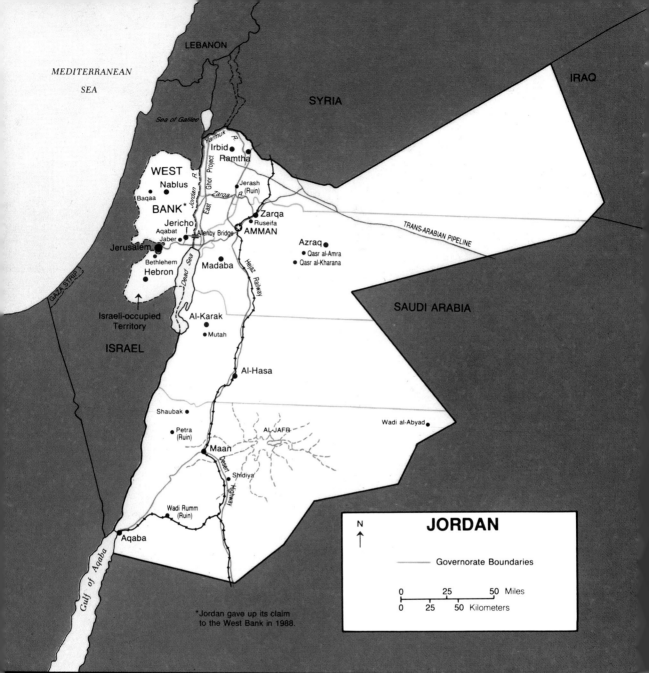

MEDITERRANEAN
SEA

LEBANON

SYRIA

IRAQ

Sea of Galilee

Yarmuk R.

Irbid
Ramtha

WEST

Nablus

Baqaa

BANK*

Jerash
(Ruin)

Jordan R.

Ghor Project

East

Zarqa

Zarqa
Ruseifa

Jericho

Aqabat
Jaber

Allenby Bridge

AMMAN

Jerusalem

Bethlehem

Hebron

GAZA STRIP

Dead Sea

Madaba

Azraq

Qasr al-Amra

Qasr al-Kharana

TRANS-ARABIAN PIPELINE

Hejaz Railway

SAUDI ARABIA

Israeli-occupied
Territory

ISRAEL

Al-Karak

Mutah

Al-Hasa

Shaubak

Petra
(Ruin)

AL-JAFR

Wadi al-Abyad

Maan

Desert Highway

Shidiya

Wadi Rumm
(Ruin)

Aqaba

Gulf of Aqaba

*Jordan gave up its claim
to the West Bank in 1988.

N

JORDAN

—— Governorate Boundaries

| 0 | 25 | 50 Miles |
| 0 | 25 | 50 Kilometers |

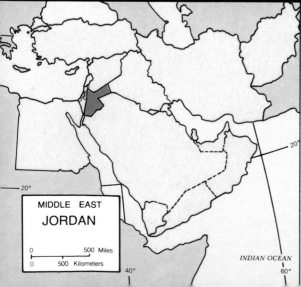

MIDDLE EAST
JORDAN

| 0 | 500 Miles |
| 0 | 500 Kilometers |

20°

40°

60°

20°

INDIAN OCEAN

METRIC CONVERSION CHART
To Find Approximate Equivalents

WHEN YOU KNOW:	MULTIPLY BY:	TO FIND:
AREA		
acres	0.41	hectares
square miles	2.59	square kilometers
CAPACITY		
gallons	3.79	liters
LENGTH		
feet	30.48	centimeters
yards	0.91	meters
miles	1.61	kilometers
MASS (weight)		
pounds	0.45	kilograms
tons	0.91	metric tons
VOLUME		
cubic yards	0.77	cubic meters
TEMPERATURE		
degrees Fahrenheit	0.56 (*after* subtracting 32)	degrees Celsius

Jordanian children display the colors of their country's flag.

Courtesy of Jordan Information Bureau, Washington, D.C.

Introduction

Since ascending the throne in 1953, King Hussein I has skillfully shaped the desert nation of Jordan, despite its location amid the political turmoil of the conflict-torn Middle East. Hussein has guided the country away from great hazards, creating a safe haven for his people in the eastern part of Palestine. Also known as the Holy Land, Palestine extends westward to the Mediterranean Sea. Despite Jordan's sometimes hostile neighbors, the country has advanced both economically and socially. Jordan's relationship with these neighbors is the most important factor in the nation's future.

Jordan is a small country, most of which is desert. Because Jordan was located on a caravan route for several centuries, many peoples have passed through the country, and each group has left its mark on the nation's history. Both ancient and modern empires—ranging from the Persian, Greek, and Roman to the more recent Ottoman and British—have shaped Jordan's destiny. Although most Jordanians share an Islamic religious background, they vary in terms of culture and ethnic heritage.

The country's Palestinians—who fled the regions now occupied by Israel as a result of the Arab-Israeli conflict—outnumber the Jordanians. Thus, Jordan faces uncertainty over which group will eventually control the country. In response to this instability, King Hussein has ensured his rule through the country's constitution— at the expense of political parties and democracy.

Independent Picture Service

The Urn, one of several tombs carved out of rock, is located near Petra's Roman amphitheater.

Courtesy of Rami Khouri/*Aramco World*

Roman emperor Antonius Pius ordered the building of this theater in Amman during the second century A.D. At that time Amman was called Philadelphia, after the Egyptian ruler who had taken the city in the third century B.C.

Jordan's Desert Patrol, also known as the Camel Corps, was established in 1931 to help settle disputes among feuding desert groups. This duty is rarely needed now, and the patrol is down to about 1,000 men.

1) The Land

The Hashemite Kingdom of Jordan is bordered on the north by Syria, on the east by Iraq, and on the southeast and south by Saudi Arabia. To the west lie Israel and an Israeli-occupied region known as the West Bank because it lies west of the Jordan River. Jordan controlled this area from 1950 until the Six-Day War in 1967, and until 1988 the nation continued to claim the area. Jordan proper, which lies east of the Jordan River, covers about 35,000 square miles and is slightly smaller than the state of Indiana. Jordan's 16 miles of coastline lie in the southwest on the Gulf of Aqaba, an arm of the Red Sea. The city of Aqaba, Jordan's only port, plays a large part in the economic life of the country.

Topography

Jordan has three major geographical regions—the Rift Valley, the Jordanian Highlands, and the Jordan Desert. The Rift Valley forms the border between Jordan and Israel (including the West Bank).

About 1,300 feet below sea level at the Dead Sea, the Rift Valley contains the lowest point on the earth. Formed millions of years ago by the sinking of the earth's crust, this deep depression is part of the Great Rift Valley, which extends from northern Syria to Mozambique in south-eastern Africa. Within Jordan, the Jordan River flows through the northern half of the Rift Valley. South of the Dead Sea, however, the valley is known as Wadi al-

Araba, and the elevation rises gradually to about 900 feet above sea level.

With an altitude of between 2,000 and 3,000 feet, the Jordanian Highlands run parallel to the Rift Valley from north of the town of Maan to the Syrian border. Chalk, sand, limestone, and flint break through the soil in the highlands. South of Maan, volcanic rocks predominate and the land is more mountainous. Wadis, or valleys that are dry most of the year, cut deeply

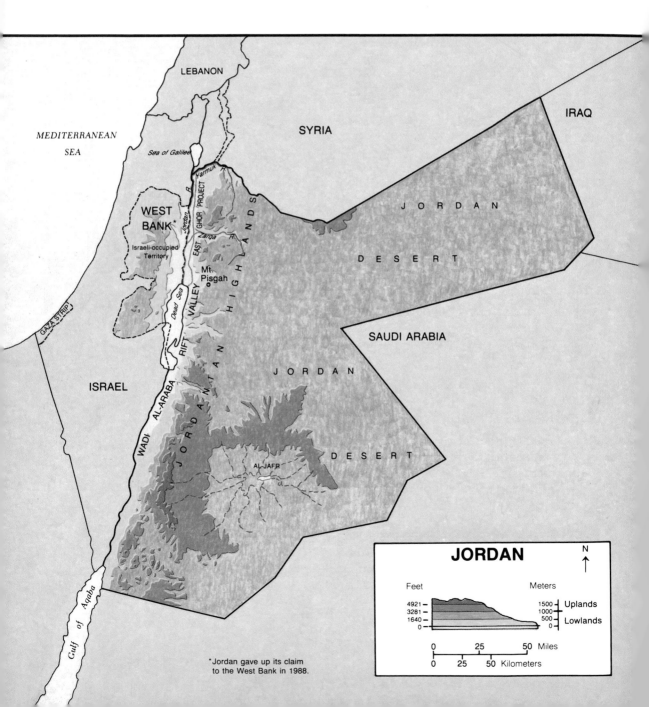

*Jordan gave up its claim
to the West Bank in 1988.

Some Bedouin families still live in the caves of Petra, as many generations of nomads have before them.

through the highlands. South of the town of Al-Karak, seasonal streams run east into a low region known as Al-Jafr.

The Jordan Desert, part of the Syrian Desert, covers 82 percent of the country, with only occasional oases—fertile areas where crops can grow. The northern section of the desert is composed of hardened lava and basalt (a dark volcanic rock), and the southern part is made of sandstone and granite, partly eroded by wind. The two types of desert meet near the town of Azraq.

Bodies of Water

The Jordan River, from which the nation takes its name, marks part of the frontier between Israel and Jordan, from the Sea of Galilee to the Dead Sea. The waterway wanders for about 200 miles, draining the waters of the Sea of Galilee, the Yarmuk River, and the surrounding streams before finally flowing into the Dead Sea. Actually a lake, the Dead Sea is 45 miles long and 10 miles wide, but its waters are 10 times saltier than the ocean.

The ancient city of Petra is glimpsed just beyond a gorge formed by steep cliffs. The Swiss explorer Johann Burckhardt rediscovered the hidden city in 1812.

11

The waters of the Jordan are valuable for irrigation. Despite attempts in the past to create a plan for the entire valley, conflicts between the Arabs and the Israelis have hindered development. As a result, the nations bordering the river—Jordan, Israel, Syria, and Lebanon—have developed their own individual schemes for using the water. In doing so they often deprive neighboring countries of water.

The East Ghor project, for example, diverts water from the Yarmuk River, a tributary of the Jordan River that is shared by Jordan and Syria, to irrigate about 30,000 acres of Jordanian agricultural land. Jordan increasingly relies on water from the Yarmuk and the Zarqa—another tributary of the Jordan—to irrigate its fields.

Climate

The climate of Jordan is generally arid, varying from pleasantly mild weather in the Jordanian Highlands to harsh desert conditions in the east. The dry season between April and October is warm and sunny with cool evenings. Daily temperatures in the capital city of Amman may range from the seventies to over 100° F during August. The contrast is even greater in the desert. Summer temperatures during the hottest part of the day average 91° F in the highlands and 104° F in the Jordan River Valley. Seasonal temperature differences are greater as distances from the Mediterranean Sea increase.

The amount of rainfall decreases farther inland, and the desert receives less than 5 inches of annual precipitation, while the

Independent Picture Service

The Dead Sea is a saltwater lake, and its heavy concentrations of minerals congeal into crusty, solid formations. Although the Dead Sea receives fresh water from the Jordan River and other, smaller streams, it has no outlet of its own. Only evaporation, aided by the hot desert climate, carries off the lake's inflow.

Courtesy of Ruth Karl

Palm trees thrive in the warm temperatures of the Gulf of Aqaba. Here, Jordan lies across from the eastern coast of Egypt's Sinai Peninsula.

highlands receive 20 or more inches in the north and 12 inches in the south. Rainfall varies greatly from year to year throughout the country, which complicates agricultural planning.

Most of the rain falls during the winter, from November to March, when the weather is cool and sometimes cold. At higher elevations winter temperatures average 15° F, while in the Jordan River Valley 57° F is the average temperature during the winter. In all regions, except the Rift Valley, frost—and sometimes snow—is fairly common. For about a month at the beginning and the end of the rainy season, hot dry air from the deserts to the south and southeast may produce strong winds called khamsins. Though these windstorms can cause much discomfort and destroy crops, they rarely last more than a day.

Goats graze on Mount Pisgah, from which Moses is said to have seen the land of Canaan (present-day Israel) beyond the Jordan River.

Independent Picture Service

13

A single date palm tree may yield as much as 600 pounds of fruit in one year. Its leaf stalks, which can be woven into bags and mats, add to the tree's economic value.

Flora and Fauna

Despite Jordan's location in the desert, flowers bloom throughout the land from February to May. Flowering plants found in Jordan include poppies, roses, irises, anemones, and wild cyclamens.

About 35,000 acres of forest exist in Jordan, and most of the trees grow on the rocky highlands. Despite heavy woodcutting by villagers and extensive grazing by flocks of sheep, the forests have been partially preserved by a reforestation program begun in 1948 by the Jordanian government. Predominant types of vegetation reflect the amount of rainfall: evergreen oaks and Aleppo pines thrive where rainfall is heaviest, grass and shrubs cover the semidry plateaus, and thorns and sparse shrubs survive in the desert. Olive trees grow wild in many places.

The oasis at Azraq provides a lush contrast to the 12,000 square miles of desert that surround it. Many species of migratory birds visit Azraq every year.

Jordan's capital since 1921, Amman is the seat of the national government as well as the kingdom's business and financial center.

The wildlife of Jordan includes both African and Asian animals—jackals, hyenas, foxes, and mongooses. Wild boars and ibex (wild goats) roam the desert. Until fairly recent times, lions and leopards stalked their prey on Jordanian soil, but these great cats are now extinct there. A curious creature is the hyrax, a small, rabbitlike animal that can climb with its hooflike claws.

Birds—including golden eagles, vultures, pigeons, and partridges—are numerous. Because of the dry climate, water-loving animals are few, but reptiles abound, including many species of snakes and lizards. Insects and their kin, such as scorpions and locusts—which have attacked crops for centuries—thrive in the dry regions.

Amman

Long before recorded history, people dwelt among the hills of Amman—the capital of Jordan—where they enjoyed the cool waters of the area's many springs. Modern Amman is a fast-growing commercial and cultural hub of the country. Its population has increased from 20,000 in 1920 to about 750,000 in the mid-1980s. The city is a famous tourist attraction originally situated among seven hills but now sprawling over several more.

Before 1875 Amman was nothing more than the ruins of the once-prosperous Roman city of Philadelphia. When Circassians immigrated to Jordan from the Caucasus region of Russia in the late nineteenth century, they settled in the area of Amman and are sometimes credited with having rebuilt the city. In 1929 Amman was declared the capital of the newly established independent nation of Transjordan.

Because Amman is a newly rebuilt city, it lacks the ancient architecture of classical Arab capitals, such as Damascus in Syria or Baghdad in Iraq. The most impressive ruin in Amman is a 2,000-year-old Roman theater, which was built in three tiers into the semicircular curve of a hill. The theater seats 6,000 spectators and is still used for outdoor festivals and orchestral concerts.

The city also lacks a native population; few inhabitants claim that they are from Amman. Rather, roughly 75 percent of the population is Palestinian, and 20,000 to 30,000 Lebanese took refuge in Amman during the peak of Lebanese conflicts in the early 1980s. The influx of refugees has forced the city to expand, creating severe shortages of housing and other community services. Nevertheless, development has exceeded expectations, and residents of Amman enjoy better facilities and employment opportunities than do many other Jordanians.

Courtesy of United Nations

Government departments and foreign companies have their offices among the original seven hills, or jebels, of Amman, though the city now stretches beyond this area.

Secondary Cities

Zarqa is Jordan's second largest city, with a population of 265,000. The major site for the nation's industrial development, Zarqa hosts an oil refinery and a tannery on

Independent Picture Service

Since the 1950s, Aqaba's appearance has changed. A three-phase plan for the city seeks to preserve the port's tourist beaches while it further expands Aqaba's industry.

Since 1959, when a phosphate loading berth was built, the port at Aqaba has expanded rapidly. It now has difficulty juggling its three functions as industrial hub, seaport, and tourist attraction.

its outskirts. The city was founded in the nineteenth century by Circassians and later became a headquarters for the Arab Legion, Jordan's army. Irbid, the third largest city (with a population of 136,200) has been an important agricultural center in ancient as well as in modern times. The opening of Yarmuk University in Irbid in 1976 boosted the city's activity.

Aqaba, situated on the Red Sea's Gulf of Aqaba, is Jordan's only seaport. Set against a rugged background of stark mountains, the city features beaches and blue waters, which attract sun-loving tourists. Aqaba is also a hub of economic activity based on its large port. New road and rail connections with Amman opened in 1978 and have boosted Aqaba's economy. During the 1980s war between Iran and Iraq the port served as the main unloading point for Iraqi war supplies.

The historic city of Madaba has many Byzantine mosaics, including this sixth-century map of Jerusalem, which is still clear enough to identify many individual buildings.

Historic Cities

Jordan has many smaller communities, several of which are renowned for their archaeological sites. Known as the Pompeii of the East, Jerash is recognized as the best and most completely preserved Greco-Roman city in southwestern Asia. In the second and third centuries A.D. Jerash thrived under Roman rule, but later the city fell into ruin. The Jordan Ministry of Tourism and Antiquities has restored several different areas, revealing hundreds of stately columns, a triumphal arch, and other splendid ruins.

Madaba dates from the middle Bronze Age (2100–1500 B.C.), but it also is noted for Byzantine mosaics from the period of Roman rule. One of Madaba's treasures is a sixth-century mosaic map of Jerusalem, the oldest map of the city, embellished with pictures of monasteries, people, boats, and plants. Other fine mosaics have been transferred to Madaba, where a museum displays depictions of Greek heroes and gods as well as exhibits of Roman jewels and utensils.

South of Madaba lies the town of Al-Karak, a crusader outpost during the twelfth century. The stronghold lay on the trade routes that led from Arabia to Egypt and the Mediterranean. Robbing caravans laden with ivory, spices, metals, jewels, and richly decorated silks became a vital source of income for the military outposts of the crusades. Al-Karak's castle-fortress, one of the most famous in the Middle East, was built by the French crusade leader Godfrey of Bouillon.

Courtesy of Jordan Information Bureau, Washington, D.C.

Jerash is believed to have been founded by Alexander the Great in the fourth century B.C., although the site has been inhabited since the late Stone Age (about 7000–4500 B.C.).

Jordan's ancient city of Petra—with its dramatic architecture and colorful history—attracts archaeologists as well as tourists.

2) History and Government

The land that is now Jordan has been sought after—and briefly possessed—by many peoples. The Assyrians and Babylonians invaded from the north, the Hittites, Romans, and Egyptians came from the west, and the Persians arrived from the east—all before the beginning of the first century A.D. Thereafter, Greeks, Arabs, Europeans, and Turks held the region in succession. The political division of Jordan from the larger area of Palestine is very recent. Jordan was historically the eastern flank of Palestine and therefore is connected to that region's history.

Early History

In about 2000 B.C., large numbers of Semitic people began to move southward, crossing the Euphrates River from northern Mesopotamia (northeastern Syria) and settling along the fertile banks of the

19

King Herod restored Jerusalem's Second Temple in the first century B.C. This model recreates the Jewish temple and city.

Jordan River. The established residents of Canaan, as Palestine was then known, called the newcomers *Ibriim* (Hebrews), which meant "the people from the other side of the river." By 1200 B.C. the Jordan River Valley was predominantly occupied by four Semitic groups—the Edomites, the Moabites, the Ammonites, and the Amorites.

Another Semitic people, the Israelites, had also lived in the region, but they left when a famine struck the land. The Israelites wandered into Egypt, where after a time they were enslaved. In about the thirteenth century B.C. a prophet named Moses led them back into Canaan. After taking Jericho and other Canaanite settlements, the Israelites settled in Palestine in the eleventh century B.C.

Three successive Israelite kings—Saul, David, and Solomon—managed to expand the kingdom of Israel well beyond its original borders and developed Jerusalem as their religious and cultural center. Solomon's reign from 961 to 922 B.C. marked the peak of Israelite strength. By 850 B.C. the kingdom had been defeated by the Moabites. In 586 B.C. Nebuchadrezzar, whose Babylonian Empire originated in southern

Mesopotamia (modern Iraq), sacked Jerusalem and exiled many of the inhabitants.

Jordan's location on caravan and military routes made it strategically important in the next several centuries. Cyrus of Per-

Roman steps and columns built in the first and second centuries A.D. lead up to the site of the early Christian cathedral built at Jerash in the fourth century.

sia (modern Iran) took the land from Nebuchadrezzar in 539 B.C. Four hundred years later the Romans occupied Syria, Jordan, and Palestine. In the first century B.C. they installed Herod the Edomite as king of Judaea (southern Palestine), giving him power over all of the major Hebrew tribes in the area.

During Herod's reign, the life of Jesus of Nazareth inspired the rise of Christianity. This new religion, though harshly suppressed by Roman emperors, eventually became the accepted faith of the empire. The Roman emperor Constantine legalized Christianity in A.D. 313. Thereafter, Christian shrines and monuments appeared throughout the territory held by the Eastern Roman, or Byzantine, Empire.

The Nabataeans and Petra

While armies invaded and occupied Jordan, an Arab people called the Nabataeans managed to hold off potential conquerors for generations. Though originally nomads, the Nabataeans constructed the secret stronghold of Petra in the cliffs of southern Jordan. Petra, still in existence today, was carved out of the sandstone walls of a canyon that can only be reached by way of a narrow gorge between 65-foot cliffs. Only the Romans, who found the source of Petra's water and dammed it, succeeded in overcoming the Nabataeans.

The Nabataeans built important trade roads guarded by forts that had been set up at strategic distances. Operating from a secure base close to the caravan routes

Part of Petra's imposing treasury building is visible near the entrance to the hidden city. The building's facade is unlike those of other Nabataean structures, leading some archaeologists to think it may have been built by the Romans in the second century A.D.

that stretched from Syria to the Arabian Peninsula, the Nabataeans grew prosperous in the fifth century, but changes in the routes of the caravans gradually halted their income. By the seventh century Petra was a dead city, its location a secret known only to Bedouin traders (a nomadic Arab people) until its rediscovery by the Swiss explorer Johann Ludwig Burckhardt in 1812.

The Muslim Conquest

After a brief period in which the Persians gained control of Jerusalem, the Arabs from the south also entered the struggle for power within Palestine. Though they had always represented potential strength, the scattered peoples of the Arabian Peninsula had lived, fought, and worshipped in small, disunited groups. In the seventh century they were united in the faith of Islam, which called for submission to the will of God as taught by the prophet Muhammad. By A.D. 636 the Arabs had conquered the Palestinian region of Jordan.

With no separation between religion and government, Islam provided the push toward a centralized political power. Taxes were collected and redistributed for the common good. Islam attempted to bring the individual, the local community, and the entire society under a single religious authority. Descendants of Muhammad automatically held positions of power. They formed a ruling class and were called *imams.*

Spurred by economic need and by the death of Muhammad in A.D. 632, the followers of Islam (called Muslims) struggled to establish Islamic supremacy and to control the profitable caravan routes. Their conquests spread Islam far to the north and east from the Arabian Peninsula as well as westward into North Africa. The Muslim conquest is one of the most influential phases in Jordanian history.

Conflict over Succession

The death of Muhammad brought about conflict among the Muslim leadership. The faithful divided over the issue of succession to power. The Shia (or Shiites) favored succession by birth; the Sunni wanted to select a new leader by vote. Assassinations occurred both between and within these opposing factions. Most of the Arab Muslims in the area now known as Jordan became Sunnis.

The Umayyad dynasty (A.D. 661–750) had its capital first in the middle of

Courtesy of Jordan Information Bureau, Washington, D.C.

Umayyad caliphs (supreme rulers of Islam) built the eighth-century Qasr al-Amra to use as a pleasure palace. The castle features beautiful paintings, whose main theme is hunting, and ornate steam baths.

Built during the Umayyad reign of the seventh century, the eight-sided Dome of the Rock in Jerusalem still stands as a symbol of the continuing Muslim presence in the Middle East. The shrine marks the place from which Muhammad is believed to have ascended to heaven.

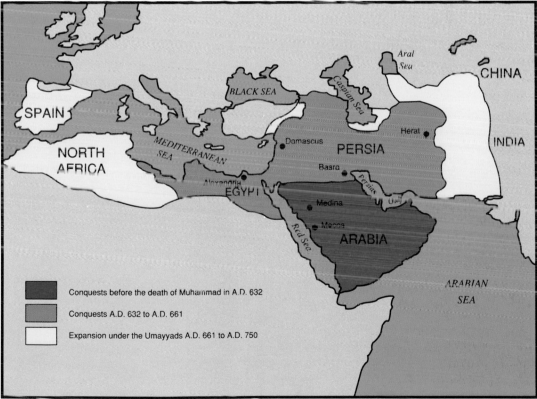

Armies made up of Muslims conquered Jordan in the first half of the seventh century. Their realm eventually stretched from Western Europe to India.

Mesopotamia and then in Damascus, Syria. The dynasty ruled according to Muslim law and was headed by a caliph who was supported by provincial governors. Muslim civil law applied only to Muslims, while separate religious communities (called *millets*) of Jews and Christians were bound by their own codes.

Successive caliphs, however, did not strictly follow the teachings of the prophet Muhammad. Though Muhammad had stressed the dignity and virtue of nomadic life, the later Umayyad caliphs developed a pampered lifestyle. Jordan, close to Damascus and the desert, became a favorite resort where traditional Arab tents were replaced by castles and elegant, costly, dome-shaped structures. In the year 750 the Abbasids, a rival Sunni group, conquered the Umayyads and moved the capital to Baghdad, Iraq.

The Crusaders

Late in the eleventh century, a new, completely foreign force came to the area—the Frankish, or Western European, crusaders. In 1095 Pope Urban II took advantage of Western fears of Muslim expansion by calling for a crusade to capture and bring the Holy Land under Christian rule. Thousands of European soldiers made their way into southwestern Asia, and Jordan and Palestine fell under European control. The crusaders built churches and Christian shrines to express their faith and castles to control the caravan routes throughout the region.

Muslims and crusaders continued to fight over the Holy Land for the next 100 years. Ultimately, Saladin, a Sunni scholar and soldier, led the Arab armies to a clear victory on the western shore of the Sea of Galilee. Possession of Jordan then passed

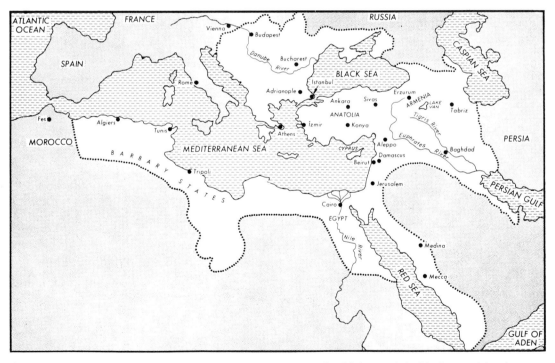

Ottoman power reached its peak in the sixteenth century under the rule of Suleyman I. At this time, social and governmental institutions that had been evolving for many years became strict codes of law. These laws were to last for almost four centuries. By the middle of the seventeenth century, the Ottoman Empire included all of the Middle East, much of the North African coast, and most of Eastern Europe. Map taken from *The Area Handbook for the Republic of Turkey*, 1973.

During a military parade, Ottoman soldiers display their horses.

briefly to Mamluk sultans, the rulers of Egypt at the time, who had helped crush the crusaders.

Turkish Domination

In the meantime, invaders from central Asia had conquered much of southwestern Asia. One group, the Ottoman Turks, had occupied Anatolia (mainland Turkey) and parts of Persia. By 1516 they had annexed Syria, Jordan, and Palestine. The Ottoman Turks, who had adopted Islam earlier, reigned as strict overlords in the region for 400 years, and social and economic development suffered from Ottoman neglect.

The Ottomans adopted a style of military government that required the least effort for the most profit. Although order was firmly enforced in the cities, areas outside the city were allowed to fall into lawlessness, and farmers beyond the protective boundaries were constantly harassed by outlaws. The Turks did not bother the raiders or the Bedouin, as long as taxes were paid. As time passed, the Turks hired desert chieftains to guard their railways, a practice the Nabataeans had used to protect their caravan lines centuries before.

The most valuable development within Jordan introduced by the Turks was the Hejaz Railway, which reached the country in 1908. Trains ran from Istanbul, Turkey, to Aleppo in Syria, over to Damascus, down to Amman, and eventually to the end of the line in Medina, a Muslim pilgrimage city in Saudi Arabia. In general, however, Turkish rule hampered the development of Palestine, Jordan, and Egypt, a handicap that persisted far into the twentieth century.

When Arab Muslims first met Western Europeans—during the crusades—there was mutual hatred and mistrust. By the early nineteenth century, however, the Arabs had been under Ottoman rule for 350 years, and the British and Russians now offered impressive new technologies.

25

The British and their allies were faced with the possibility of war not only in Europe but against the Turks in Palestine as well. The Arabs represented a possible foothold in the region. Thus, the Arabs and the British had something to offer each other, and slowly communication was established between them.

Arab Response to Turkish Policies

Arab dissatisfaction with Ottoman rule grew in the early 1900s. In 1908 a Turkish nationalist group called the Committee of Union and Progress forced the Ottoman sultan Abdulhamid II to restore constitutional rule. The following year they deposed him. This nationalist group, later known as the Young Turks, opposed government tolerance of millets—separate religious communities for minorities. The Young Turks wanted to absorb other cultures into that of the Turks.

The Arabs responded in two major ways to the policies of the Young Turks. First, Arab intellectuals in Lebanon and Syria began to work toward Arab freedom within the Ottoman Empire. Because the Young Turks had increased military pressure in an effort to slow the rise of Arab resistance, secret societies were founded, most notably the Young Arab Society. These groups published underground pamphlets and posters calling for an end to foreign control of Palestine and the Arabian Peninsula.

Second, working essentially outside of Ottoman rule, the remote desert groups of Jordan and Arabia stepped up their efforts to disrupt Ottoman trade. Though these groups had no unified political voice, they helped to weaken the economic base of the empire.

In 1914 Hussein ibn Ali—the grand emir (prince) of Mecca and a sharif, or direct descendant of Muhammad—came forward to serve as a link between Arabs of the cities and the desert societies. After negotiating with Arabs in Syria and Lebanon

Abdullah *(top)*, son of Sharif Hussein, sought British aid against Ottoman rule from Lord Horatio Kitchener *(above)*. As the organizer of British forces during World War I, Lord Kitchener enlisted Arab support. In return, the British promised the Arabs independence.

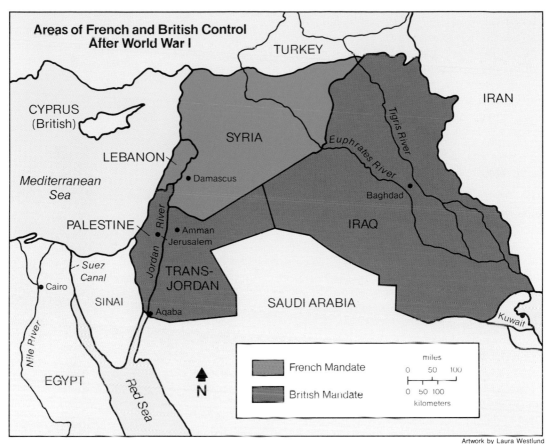

Areas of French and British Control
After World War I

TURKEY

IRAN

CYPRUS
(British)

SYRIA

LEBANON

Mediterranean
Sea

Euphrates River

Tigris River

• Damascus

Baghdad

PALESTINE

Jordan River

• Amman
Jerusalem

IRAQ

TRANS-
JORDAN

Suez
Canal

• Cairo

SINAI

• Aqaba

SAUDI ARABIA

Kuwait

Nile River

EGYPT

Red Sea

N

French Mandate

British Mandate

miles
0   50   100

0 50 100
kilometers

Artwork by Laura Westlund

After World War I, Britain and France divided much of the Middle East into British and French mandates, or areas of influence. During the mandate period, the British oversaw the establishment of an Arab government in Transjordan.

through various secret organizations, Sharif Hussein was accepted as the spokesperson for the northern societies.

British Influence

Hussein's son, Abdullah, approached a British representative in Cairo, Lord Horatio Kitchener, for aid in defeating the Ottomans. Lord Kitchener did not initially give Hussein much hope of British assistance. At the outset of World War I in 1914, however, Kitchener was promoted to secretary of war and sought Arab support against the Turks.

In exchange for Arab agreement to fight the Turks openly, Britain's high commissioner Sir Henry MacMahon promised

Sharif Hussein territory for Arab independence under a "Sharifian Arab government." A number of letters exchanged by MacMahon and Hussein—called the MacMahon letters—set up rough boundaries for this area.

On June 5, 1916, Hussein led the Arab Revolt against Ottoman rule. His sons, Abdullah and Faisal, along with other prominent sheikhs (chiefs), led desert forces from Jordan and Arabia. With money, arms, and technical advisers (the most famous of whom was T. E. Lawrence, or Lawrence of Arabia) from Great Britain, Hussein succeeded in stopping traffic along the Hejaz Railway. In October, he was able to proclaim himself king of the Arabs.

During the Arab Revolt of 1916, Wadi Rumm served as a base from which T. E. Lawrence (Lawrence of Arabia) raided Turkish outposts. The desert landscape of this region is home to the Huwayat people, who claim to be descendants of Muhammad, the founder of Islam.

THE BALFOUR DECLARATION

The British had also negotiated support during World War I from the Zionist (Jewish) immigrants located in Palestine. A movement called Zionism had begun in the late nineteenth century to establish a Jewish homeland. Theodor Herzl had formed the World Zionist Organization and called for Jews to immigrate to Palestine, site of the ancient kingdom of Israel.

Discussions took place in November 1917 between the British foreign secretary Arthur James Balfour and the Zionists. Together they produced a document known as the Balfour Declaration, which promised British assistance in the creation of a home for Jews in Palestine. Arab opposition to this Jewish homeland died down after the British assured the Arabs that no people in Palestine would be governed by any other people.

THE SYKES-PICOT AGREEMENT

Arab fears of outside control of the area were raised again in November 1917, when the Bolshevik (Russian) regime made public a secret agreement between the French and British governments. Although the Sykes-Picot Agreement made plans for an Arab state on the Arabian Peninsula, it also called for the territory of Palestine to be divided between Great Britain and France. Britain again reassured Arab leaders, and the Allied war effort came to a conclusion in 1917 when Britain captured Jerusalem and when troops led by Faisal, Hussein's son, took Damascus, Syria. The armistice with Turkey was signed on October 31, 1918.

Emir Faisal established an independent Arab government in October 1918 at Damascus. At the international conference held in San Remo, Italy, in 1920, however, France and Great Britain divided Syria,

Palestine, and what would become Transjordan between themselves. French troops forced Faisal to leave the country in July 1920.

Formation of Transjordan

The British tried to fulfill promises made in the MacMahon letters. Winston Churchill, who was the British secretary for the colonies at the time, reserved a portion of Palestine for Arab rule, though the British were to remain in military and supervisory roles. Thus, the East Bank of the Jordan River became known as Transjordan (Beyond the Jordan), while the West Bank remained a British administrative colony. Because a majority of the desert societies supported the Hussein family, the British named Hussein's son Abdullah ruler of Transjordan in 1921. Transjordanian independence was declared on May 15, 1923, though the British remained effectively in control.

The British supplied development funds and helped Abdullah raise and train a national fighting force called the Arab Legion. Through a series of treaties, Transjordan moved closer to complete independence. The West Bank, on the other hand, under full British control, had become a place of great tension by the mid-1930s. Thousands of Jews had begun to immigrate to Palestine from Germany as Nazi restrictions against Jews spread. Arabs on both sides of the river were alarmed at the increase in the Jewish population.

The Arab-Israeli Conflict

Tensions between Arabs and Jews increased, and in 1947 the British government asked the United Nations (UN) to help solve the problem. According to the plan devised by the UN, Palestine was divided into two states—Arab and Jewish – and Jerusalem was to be put under international control. The British withdrew from Palestine, and the Jews proclaimed the independent State of Israel on May 14, 1948. Immediately thereafter, the Arab nations of Egypt, Syria, Transjordan, Lebanon, Iraq, Saudi Arabia, and the Yemens attacked the Jewish state.

A period illustration depicts Lawrence of Arabia in traditional Arab dress. The British soldier and author disliked military formalities. Here, he stands barefoot with arms folded as uniformed officers salute and march around him.

Courtesy of Jordan Information Bureau, Washington, D.C.

Israel defeated the combined Arab forces and gained strategic territory along its borders. But Transjordan's Arab Legion took central Palestine (the West Bank) and captured the Old City of Jerusalem, which contained many ancient Muslim holy sites. The Jordanian legislature formally authorized the annexation of the West Bank in 1950. In the same year, Transjordan was renamed the Hashemite Kingdom of Jordan after its founding dynasty, the Hashemites, who, under the leadership of Sharif Hussein, had revolted against the Ottoman Empire.

With the annexation of the West Bank and the influx of refugees into Jordan, thousands of Palestinians—who were granted Jordanian citizenship—were added to the Hashemite Kingdom's voting population. This new faction began to push for a limit to the power of the king and the cabinet, pressing for control by popular vote. In 1950 Palestinians were further angered by news that King Abdullah had negotiated with Israel. A year later Abdullah was assassinated by a Palestinian.

The crown passed to Abdullah's second son, Talal, who resigned shortly thereafter

Jordan's flag is derived from a similar version that was introduced in 1917 by Sharif Hussein. His son, Abdullah, king of Transjordan, changed the order of the colors and added the seven-pointed star on a red field. The star represents the first seven verses of the Koran.

because of mental illness. Talal's son, Hussein ibn Talal, whom Abdullah had seen as his successor, was declared King Hussein I on August 11, 1952, and assumed constitutional duties in 1953 after reaching 18 years of age.

Threats to Hussein's Reign

Amid increased tensions between Jordan and its neighbors during the first years of Hussein's authority, Jordan joined the UN in 1955. With Palestinians making up about two-thirds of Jordan's population, mass demonstrations continued to threaten Hussein's authority. To ease tensions within his country, Hussein expelled the British commander of the Arab Legion. The move meant eventual loss of British funds, but it strengthened Hussein's bond with other Arab leaders.

The sheikh of a local Bedouin group entertains Jordan's Desert Patrol, first with camel races and then with a feast of spicy meat and rice.

Yasir Arafat founded the commando group Al-Fatah in 1956. In 1968, four years after Al-Fatah was linked with the Palestine Liberation Organization (PLO), Arafat became PLO chairperson.

A soldier keeps watch in this no-man's-land—an area in Jerusalem that was patrolled from 1948 to 1967.

Courtesy of UNRWA

After the Arab-Israeli conflict of June 1967, a temporary bridge linked eastern Jordan with the West Bank. Months after the fighting, thousands of refugees continued to cross into Jordan.

Nevertheless, radical Arab nationalists, who called for a Palestinian revolt and for revenge against Israel, increased opposition to Hussein's rule throughout the next decade. But the king retained control through the loyal Jordanian Arab Army (formerly the Arab Legion) and through support from Western nations.

Growing Tensions

In 1964 the Palestinians began to unite under a new force—the Palestine Liberation Organization (PLO)—whose purpose was to oppose Israel and to work for the return of Palestine to the Palestinians. The Palestine National Charter, drawn up by Palestinians at a conference in 1964, forbade the PLO to interfere in the internal affairs of any Arab country. Almost immediately, however, trouble developed in Jordan.

Jordan possessed many large encampments of Palestinian refugees from Israel, and the PLO moved freely within this population, attempting to tax Palestinians, to train soldiers, and to distribute arms in the villages. When the Palestinian guerrilla organization Al-Fatah was added to the PLO in 1964, the combined forces began to launch secret strikes against Israel from within Jordan. Israel

33

Participating in a colorful procession, members of the Jordanian Arab Army are outfitted in much the same way as their predecessors, who, until 1956, were known as the Arab Legion. The heart of the original army was composed of a small number of soldiers who had fought in the Arab Revolt of 1916.

developed a policy of massive retaliation —destroying Arab settlements along the Jordanian border. In response, Hussein signed a military alliance with Egypt on May 30, 1967.

In the Six-Day War that followed in June 1967, Israel defeated Egypt, Jordan, and Syria and won the West Bank and all of Jerusalem from Jordan. Jordan lost, thereby, an estimated one-third of its best agricultural land and its major tourist centers, and some 200,000 additional refugees fled to the East Bank. The UN Relief and Works Agency (UNRWA), which had been set up in 1949 after the first Arab-Israeli war, supplied Jordan with funds and services to meet the needs of the Palestinian refugees.

Civil War

Though the loss of the West Bank posed an economic problem for Jordan, the most pressing concern following the 1967 Six-Day War was the growing power of guerrilla groups connected to the PLO. Because many of these Palestinians—who represented over half of Jordan's population— had previously been granted Jordanian citizenship, the conflict took on the proportions of a civil war. By August 1970 fighting had broken out between the guerrillas and the Jordanian army, and a PLO faction had hijacked and blown up three European airliners. As a result, King Hussein ordered the Jordanian army to suppress the guerrillas.

In fighting that continued through most of September 1970, which became known as Black September, the PLO and other groups were defeated and driven from the capital of Amman and from most of the country. Despite continued opposition from guerrilla groups over the next year, Jordanian forces captured the last of the PLO bases.

Courtesy of Munir Nasr/UNRWA

The UN Relief and Works Agency (UNRWA) has set up huge refugee camps on the West Bank and in Jordan. As of 1982, over 400,000 Palestinians were registered as refugees.

Courtesy of Steve Feinstein

Refugee camps are located in western Jordan. Unlike other Arab states, Jordan is the only country in the region that has granted citizenship to Palestinians. Nevertheless, many Palestinians have chosen to remain in the camps because they still consider Palestine to be their true homeland.

Dressed in guerrilla gear, a young member of the PLO receives instruction on how to handle his weapon. When PLO guerrilla fighters launched attacks against Israel from Jordan during the late 1960s, Israeli counterattacks put pressure on King Hussein to support the PLO. His refusal prompted frequent clashes with the PLO and led to civil war in 1970.

Photo by UPI/Bettmann Newsphotos

Many of the guerrillas were pursued into Lebanon, where they tried to continue their operations. A radical wing, led by PLO chairman Yasir Arafat, named itself Black September in recognition of Palestinians killed in the September fighting. Black September was responsible for several hijackings over the next two years.

During the Yom Kippur War of 1973—so called because the Arab surprise attack against Israel was launched on that Jewish holy day—Jordan sent only a few brigades to the aid of Egypt and Syria, an indication of Jordan's confidence in its own

security. The end of the war brought Jordan the return of funds from oil-rich Arab neighbors, most notably from Kuwait. These funds had been cut off in the late 1950s in response to Jordan's failure to back several decisions of the Arab League, a council of the leaders of the Arab nations.

Dispute over the West Bank

Jordan's economy continued to grow in the 1970s as funds from Kuwait, Saudi Arabia, and the United States reduced debts caused by Palestinian refugees and the war effort. The situation was further eased by the establishment of an "open bridges" policy between Israeli West Bank and Jordanian East Bank communities. Many Palestinians returned to the West Bank when it became safe to do so.

Relatively secure for the first time since 1953, King Hussein turned his attention to solving the problem of a homeland for the Palestinians. In 1972 Hussein had proposed a federation plan to join the East and West banks under the name United Arab Kingdom, with a single capital at Amman. The reaction of the Arab world had been hostile. The move was seen as an attempt by Hussein to take control of land that rightfully belonged to independent Palestinians. In 1974 at the Arab summit conference in Rabat, Morocco, the PLO—not Jordan, as Hussein had hoped—was named the official representative group for the Palestinians.

After the Rabat summit, Hussein officially stood by the decisions reached there. He supported several peace proposals, always maintaining that the PLO must be involved as representatives of the Palestinian people.

Unofficially, however, Hussein embraced measures aimed at strengthening Jordan's claim as caretaker of the West Bank. In 1984 he reconvened the Jordanian Parliament, half of whose members came from the West Bank. In March 1986 the Jordanian legislature increased the number of seats in the house of representatives from 60 to 142 (71 seats each for the East and West banks). Six months later Hussein revealed a plan to invest $1.3 billion to reconstruct the West Bank and the disputed Gaza Strip, a tiny piece of land

The Allenby Bridge provides passage between Jordan and the West Bank. For many Palestinian refugees, the bridge is one of the only links to friends and relatives living in Jerusalem.

37

along the Mediterranean between Israel and Egypt.

In late 1987, a Palestinian *intifadeh* (uprising) broke out in the Israeli-occupied territories. The frequent clashes that occurred between Israeli soldiers and Palestinians in 1988 brought the two opponents no closer to any settlement. In August 1988, Hussein gave up official claim to the West Bank, thereby opting out of a direct role in negotiations. The move meant that the Palestinians living in the region would lose Jordanian development funds and government jobs, and it left the PLO as the only representative of the Palestinian people.

Government

In accordance with the Constitution of 1952, Jordan is headed by a hereditary monarch, who has power over the executive, legislative, and judicial branches of the government. The monarch appoints a council of ministers—which is led by a prime minister—to assist with executive duties. The monarch also signs and executes all laws, declares war, concludes peace, commands the armed forces, and approves amendments to the constitution. Although political parties have been banned since 1963, King Hussein promotes national unity by bringing opposition leaders into the government.

The bicameral (two-house) Parliament forms the legislative branch. The members of the house of representatives are elected to four-year terms by citizens who are 18 years of age or older. Women voted for the first time in 1984. In 1988 King Hussein removed all West Bank employees from the government payroll. This reduced the size of the house of representatives by half. The monarch appoints the members of the senate, whose delegates hold office for eight-year terms. Most of the seats in Parliament are reserved for Muslims.

The Jordanian judicial system consists of three kinds of courts. The first type

Courtesy of Jordan Information Bureau, Washington, D.C.

King Hussein is a direct descendant of Muhammad through the prophet's daughter Fatima.

is made up of civil courts. Magistrates' courts, the lowest in the civil system, hear minor criminal and civil cases. More important cases being tried for the first time go to courts of first instance. At the top of the ladder is the supreme court, which presides over cases against the state, hears appeals, and interprets the law.

The second category is made up of religious courts for both Muslims and non-Muslims. These courts rule on personal matters, such as marriage and divorce. The third category consists of special courts, such as land, government, property, municipal, custom, and tax courts. All judges for the judiciary are appointed, and are sometimes dismissed, by the monarch.

Jordan is divided into five administrative units called governorates. A governor appointed by the monarch heads each district. Governors have sole authority for all government departments and development projects in their respective areas. In the cities, mayors and their elected councils take care of local affairs.

These smiling children live in the Jordan Valley, where farmers planted wheat and barley as long as 10,000 years ago.

3) The People

Major population shifts have resulted from warfare and economic upheavals within Jordan. In addition, only two censuses—in 1961 and in 1979—have ever been conducted in the country. Thus, the nation's population is difficult to measure. In 1988 the population estimate for the country was 3.8 million.

Most of the nation's people are Arabs who speak Arabic. Nevertheless, tensions exist between groups with differing ideologies. One of the most important power struggles is between the Bedouin—the original inhabitants of the country—and the Palestinians, who now represent over 60 percent of the population.

Despite these ethnic conflicts, the Jordanian government seeks to foster national loyalty and social change. Projects have been initiated to raise the standard of living by improving housing, education, and medical care. In spite of jealousies, constant intrigues, and the influx of refugees, social improvements have proceeded.

Women meet at a station *(right)* to gather the day's supply of water. The tents that served as their dwellings have since been replaced by sturdier, but still temporary, concrete block structures *(below)*.

Courtesy of George Nehmeh/UNRWA

Courtesy of UNRWA

UNRWA's play centers give refugee children the opportunity for organized recreational activities.

Courtesy of George Nehmeh/UNRWA

The customary desert life of the Bedouin still centers on their herds of camels, goats, and sheep. A Bedouin child soon acquires long-held values, such as respect for the advice of the elders of the group and deep regard for the rights of neighbors.

Palestinians

The arrival of refugees has altered the population of Jordan, affecting the nation's social, political, and business life. Approximately 700,000 refugees were living in Jordan in 1966, and 350,000 more arrived after the Six-Day War in 1967. Many Palestinians have since moved out of the refugee camps, and they now make significant contributions to the country's well-being.

Other Palestinians, however, continue to live in poverty under unsanitary conditions. Some have small, sturdy houses within the camp areas; others live in tents. Schools, clinics, and other health facilities have been built near some of the camps.

Since most of the inhabitants of the camps insist on returning eventually to their homeland, they are classified as displaced persons and resist efforts at resettlement. The UNRWA, with international financial assistance, has supplied most of the funding for social programs for these refugees.

Bedouin

Although the Bedouin actually represent only a small percentage of the Jordanian population, they have enjoyed a strong political and cultural role in Jordan. They are loyal to King Hussein and make up a high percentage of the Jordanian army. Perhaps because Bedouin are sometimes viewed as the original Arabs, East Bank Jordanians uphold the Bedouin lifestyle as a model for all Jordanians to follow.

The Bedouin live primarily in the eastern two-thirds of Jordan, a desert region that stretches from Jordan's Syrian and Iraqi frontiers in the north to its Saudi Arabian border in the south. They may also be found in the western portion—including Amman—at some times of the year. Although they are classified as nomads, Bedouin groups have fixed winter and summer campgrounds—areas that they return to each year. Furthermore, as they take up agriculture and participate more in the cash economy of Jordan, many Bedouin are developing more settled living patterns.

Three of the largest Bedouin groups are the Bani Sukhurs, the Huwaytats, and the Sirhans. Once they were all camel herders, but now some of them have added sheep and goats to their flocks. All three groups share the traditions of desert life, which include courtesy, courage, and hospitality.

The pattern of Bedouin life varies according to the size of the group. Some units consist of only a few families, or of a father, the families of his sons, and his unmarried daughters. Groups like the Bani Sukhur may have 2,000 to 3,000 interrelated families, all of whom owe family

Courtesy of Zachary J. Marell

An Arab woman wearing a traditional head veil and long dress shops at a suq, or outdoor market.

allegiance to a sheikh, the ruling head of the family. In such a large tribe there may be as many as a dozen sheikhs.

Education

The rapid development taking place in Jordan requires a high standard of education. No longer do family and social status completely determine the future of an aspiring youth. Jordan has not yet become a society where people of all backgrounds can advance on their merits alone, but many leadership positions cannot be maintained without specialized education. For most Jordanians, education has become a status symbol and a source of social prestige. Although only 32 percent of the population was literate in 1961, that figure rose to 70 percent by 1985.

Courtesy of Jordan Information Bureau, Washington, D.C.

Many women, like these three students at the University of Jordan, now dress in Western-style fashions.

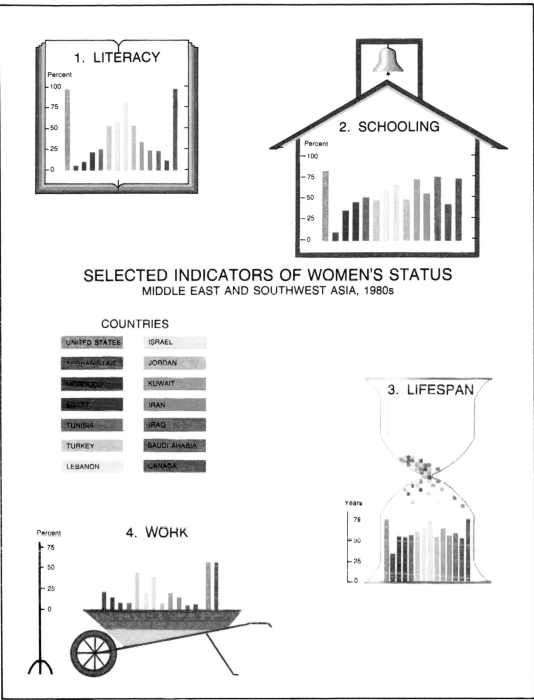

Artwork by Carol F. Barrett

Depicted in this chart are factors relating to the status of women in the Middle East and southwest Asia. Graph 1, labeled Literacy, shows the percentage of adult women who can read and write. Graph 2 illustrates the proportion of school-aged girls who actually attend elementary and secondary schools. Graph 3 depicts the life expectancy of female babies at birth. Graph 4 shows the percentage of women in the income-producing work force. Data taken from *Women in the World: An International Atlas*, 1986 and from *Women . . . A World Survey*, 1985.

Young students play music together at Amman's Haya Arts Center. For children ages 6 to 14, the center also offers such classes as drama and sculpture.

Primary education is free and compulsory for all children. The Ministry of Education runs most of the schools, establishes the curricula, and sets the state examinations throughout the system. Six years of elementary and three years of preparatory (lower secondary) studies are required. Young Jordanians who seek further education continue secondary school and may prepare to attend a university.

The University of Jordan in Amman has offered courses in science, economics and

These Bedouin schoolboys are just getting used to a settled way of life in a new village.

Courtesy of Jordan Information Bureau, Washington, D.C.

Schoolboys participate in an activity during recess at one of Jordan's elementary schools.

commerce, medicine, and Islamic law since 1962. Yarmuk University in Irbid was opened in 1976, and a third university opened in the mid-1980s at Mutah, near Al-Karak.

Unlike most Middle Eastern universities, those schools are patterned after those in the United States rather than those in Europe. Although the Jordanian universities are relatively new, they are considered by some to be the best state-supported institutions of higher learning in the Arab Middle East. Many vocational schools, including nursing and military institutes and private and missionary schools, operate in addition to the universities.

Literature and Music

Jordanians, like other Arabs, consider literature—in the forms of prose, poetry, and conversation—to be the highest creative pursuit. They idealize the Arabic language and honor those who speak it eloquently. Because the Koran, the Muslim book of holy writings, is upheld as the perfect expression of Arabic, its traditional writing style has greatly influenced literature. Nevertheless, both modern adaptations of classical Arab forms and Western literary models are gaining acceptance.

By the mid-twentieth century a growing sense of nationalism found literary expression. The new attitude was spurred on by strong feelings against both foreign domination and the Zionist movement. Ibrahim Tuqan became one of the most popular nationalist poets of the period. He influenced his sister Fawda Tuqan, who went on to become one of Jordan's outstanding poets. More recent literary topics have included the Arab-Israeli conflict, PLO guerrilla resistance, and the plight of Palestinian refugees.

Courtesy of Jordan Information Bureau, Washington, D.C.

Some of the crafts a tourist might find at a shop like this one in Amman include jewelry, wood carvings, and woven rugs.

Closely interwoven with poetry, traditional Arabic music is highly improvisational and often is based on a five-tone —rather than the Western eight-tone— scale. Instrumentalists accompany vocalists rather than performing nonvocal music. Some of the most common classical instruments include the oud, a plucked instrument with 9 to 11 strings; the kemancha, an Arabic violin made from a gourd, usually with only 1 string; and the nay, which resembles the flute.

Handicrafts

Jordanian artisans employ techniques that blend methods as old as the Bronze Age and as new as power-driven drills. Reflecting the long influence of Islam—which forbids representations of the human body —designs used in carving, metalwork, and embroidery are mainly plant, flower, animal, and geometric motifs. Other designs,

Courtesy of Jordan Information Bureau, Washington, D.C.

Jordan's Ministry of Education provides specialized vocational training at women's craft centers such as this one in the Jordan Valley. Vocational courses take two to three years to complete.

Two Arab women dress in richly embroidered skirts and head veils. Each also wears the traditional face veil, which may be as decorative as gold jewelry.

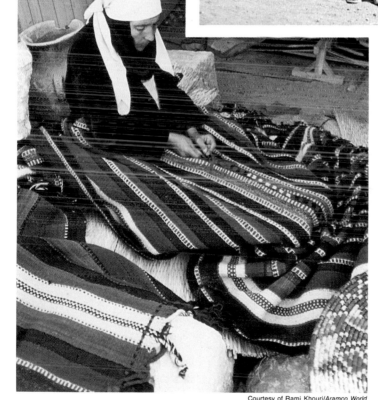

Rug weaving is one of the oldest crafts practiced in Jordan. Using goats' hair mixed with sheep's wool, a woman weaves a vividly striped rug—the style traditionally used to cover a tent floor.

however, reflect Christian traditions, such as crosses and images of saints. Proverbs delicately engraved in Arabic and English are often part of the design.

Wood carving is a flourishing industry that caters to both tourists and local people. Most of the carvings are made from olive wood, and the finished objects are polished by hand with beeswax, varnish, or plastic coating.

Metalwork, such as costume jewelry and religious objects, may be made of silver, gold, or bronze. Goldsmiths work outside their shops and stalls at bazaars (street markets) using techniques handed down from generation to generation. Traditionally, mosaics adorn the walls and floors of both village dwellings and modern homes.

Most carpets for local trade are made of sheepskin and are used by Bedouin to cover the ground in their tents. Sheepskin rugs are washable, very strong, do not fade, and last for years. Villagers make rugs in bright wools from goat and camel threads that have been dyed in many colors. In Al-Karak and Shaubak—hubs of rug making that cater to tourists—the designs are more Western.

Intricately patterned rugs surround a Bedouin man and his son. The bright, geometric designs are still used for decorating, as they have been for hundreds of years.

Onlookers gather to watch camel racers at a track near Amman.

Festivals

In big cities and in villages, weddings call for dances and a festival that lasts for several days. Special songs accompany all occasions—births, funerals, weddings, plowing, planting, and harvesting. The festivals for harvesting include traditional rituals. Jordanians would not harvest without them, and the entire family, including relatives, takes part.

Many dances begin with the pounding of feet on the floor to mark the rhythm—this is called the *debkah*. The dance known

A woman in elaborate costume performs the *debkah*, Jordan's most popular folk dance.

Independent Picture Service

as the *sahjeh* is performed by Bedouin, and the Circassians have their own sword dance. The government has formed a national Circassian troupe that performs in local villages and on television and whose songs are played on the radio.

Religion

The vast majority of Jordan is Muslim—over 90 percent of the population is made up of Sunni Muslims, whose institutions receive governmental support. This Muslim religious base is reflected in the country's Constitution of 1952, which states that the king and his successors must be Muslims, born of Muslim parents.

Eight percent of Jordan's population is Christian. Christians are mostly of the Eastern Orthodox and Greek Catholic sects, followed in number by Roman Catholics and Protestants. A small number of Druze—a secretive sect that branched off from Islam—live near the Syrian border, along with Samaritans and Circassians. The Samaritans are descendants of an ancient Jewish sect, and the Circassians are Sunni Muslims.

Islam, the predominant faith, is based on five religious duties, called *arkan*, or pillars. The first pillar is called *shahada*, or

The ancient art of falconry—hunting with trained hawks—is still practiced in Jordan.

Independent Picture Service

49

An engraving shows al-Haram, the most sacred mosque in Mecca, and thousands of pilgrims making the hajj. The building covered with black cloth in the courtyard of the mosque is the Kaaba, believed to have been built by the prophet Abraham, from whom both Muslims and Jews claim descent.

recitation of the creed: "there is no God but Allah and Muhammad is his prophet." Salat (daily prayer), the second pillar, is satisfied by turning toward Mecca and praying five times each day: at dawn, noon, midafternoon, sunset, and nightfall.

The third duty is called zakat, or alms-giving, which is a property tax that supports those who are crippled or poor.

Sawm (fasting), the fourth pillar, requires every Muslim to fast from sunrise to sunset during the holy month of Ramadan.

The fifth and final pillar of Islam is the most difficult. The hajj, a journey to the holy city of Mecca in Saudi Arabia, is required once in a lifetime. Every Muslim who is able, regardless of the distance or difficulty, makes the pilgrimage.

Monasteries are home to some of Jordan's minority Christian population.

Food

Jordanian cuisine is hearty and satisfying. In Aqaba charcoal-broiled and highly seasoned fish—especially shrimp and lobster caught in the Red Sea—is popular. Jordanians enjoy *mansif,* which is a Bedouin dish of lamb, yogurt, and rice that is cooked long and simmered well.

Dinner in a wealthy Jordanian home may begin with appetizers, such as small shish kebabs, roasted sardines, and tiny meatballs. The meal itself may start with a cup of spicy soup that combines lamb broth, onions, and green peppers. This first course may be followed by mansif, thick chick-peas, or roasted lamb. Beef is rarely eaten because cattle are too useful as work animals to slaughter them. The dessert may be chocolate pudding, a very sweet coconut dish, or a pastry, followed by fresh fruit and thick, dark Bedouin coffee.

Although there is a Muslim restriction against alcohol, some Jordanians enjoy beer—which is often served with olives and nuts at any time of the day. Jordanians delight in cold drinks. Small clay barrels hold homemade fruit concoctions, sold in stalls in every city and hamlet. These beverages are made from papayas, sugarcane, pineapples, oranges, and lemons.

An important export crop, tomatoes are also sold locally and are used in many Jordanian dishes.

Bedouin hosts instruct a guest from the city in the proper way to eat *mansif.*

51

Health

In 1950 the Ministry of Health was established to plan for the long-term development of medical care and facilities. Health services have improved steadily since that time, especially in Amman. Although services are not nearly as good in rural areas, an increased enrollment in medical training programs during the 1980s is expected to improve the situation.

A national health insurance plan covers medical, dental, and eye care at a very modest cost. Those who cannot afford such care are treated free. Hospitals and clinics serve Amman and all the larger cities. The villages are supplied with rural medical services and visiting nurses. Malaria and most infectious diseases have been brought under control with the help of vaccines.

Tuberculosis (TB) is one of the main public health problems facing the nation. As nomadic Bedouin—who previously have not been exposed to TB—settle in towns, many of them contract the disease because they have no resistance to it. The govern-

Courtesy of Jordan Information Bureau, Washington, D.C.

At the Zarqa Main hot springs near the Dead Sea, Jordanians camp, relax, and take in the healing waters.

Physically handicapped children receive special care and artificial aids at this children's hospital. About half of the children in the program are Palestinian refugees, whose treatment is funded by the UNRWA.

ment has taken active measures to combat and prevent the spread of this painful and sometimes deadly lung ailment.

The Ministry of Health has upgraded an old school of nursing into a college to train nurses. Graduates from the college work for the ministry as visiting nurses. The Ministry of Defense has a similar institution whose graduates work in the hospitals of the Jordanian army. The UNRWA sponsors medical clinics in all the refugee camps.

Jordanian life expectancy averages 69 years, which is high for western Asia. The infant mortality rate of 56 deaths per 1,000 live births compares well with most other countries in western Asia, but it is not as good as the North American average of 10 deaths for every 1,000 live births. Based on the population growth rate for

1988, the number of Jordanians will double in 19 years —one of the fastest growth rates in western Asia.

A bus picks up mothers and children on their way to one of Jordan's health-care clinics.

At a brick manufacturing plant near Amman, a crane lifts slabs made from lime and silicate (metal salts).

4) The Economy

With only new industry, few natural resources, and land that is largely too dry for crop raising, Jordan is just beginning to support itself financially. The nation depends heavily on aid from foreign countries, especially from oil-rich Arab nations, such as Saudi Arabia and Kuwait.

In the decade before the 1967 war, Jordan's economy grew rapidly. Although Israeli occupation of the West Bank initially impaired the country's development, Jordan has since made up for this handicap, and its economy has continued to expand. Furthermore, the migration of Palestinians to the East Bank stimulated a construction boom and eventually provided Jordan with a more skilled labor force, since the refugees had been accustomed to a more urban society on the West Bank.

Thus, the post-1967 view that Jordan could not survive economically without the West Bank has given way to a more optimistic outlook. King Hussein has officially given up the Jordanian claim to the West Bank, and he has successfully pursued East Bank development. The nation's gross domestic product (GDP)—the amount of goods and services produced in the country—has increased in real terms each year since 1970.

Agriculture

Although Jordan is composed largely of desert, its major economic activities are farming and livestock raising, which occupy about 20 percent of the population. As a result, Jordanian agriculture is unstable because a large proportion of the total agricultural output comes from dry farming in areas that have numerous droughts. Special emphasis has been given to irrigation schemes as well as to soil and water projects that will increase production of drought-resistant crops in areas where irrigation is not possible.

Increased cultivation has rewarded the Ministry of Agriculture's efforts to replace traditional farming methods with modern equipment, fertilizers, and irrigation systems. Annual fruit and vegetable production has risen steadily since the 1950s. Tomatoes, eggplants, olives, wheat, and

A Bedouin shepherd tends his flock near Irbid. In the background, land has been shaped to combat soil erosion.

Courtesy of M. Gaieb/FAO

Young olive plants are grown under ideal greenhouse conditions at a research station near Amman. Outside of the greenhouse, agricultural projects often include various methods of irrigation. This approach to land use is needed in order to offset Jordan's extremely dry climate.

citrus fruits are the leading crops. Melons, cabbages, cucumbers, and rice are the most popular foods for Jordanians, and nuts are also a major crop. By encouraging farmers to produce more wheat, barley, onions, and potatoes, the country has decreased its costs for food imports, and some fruits and vegetables are exported to other countries. Livestock—which includes sheep, goats, cattle, and camels—is concentrated in the desert.

Mining

Jordan's most important minerals are phosphate and potash, both of which are used in fertilizers. Two very small oil wells near the Saudi Arabian and Iraqi borders are producing substantial amounts, but the extent of their reserves is unknown. The Dead Sea contains many dissolved minerals, and potash and magnesium are extracted from its waters. Clays, copper ore, and silica (used in the manufacturing of glass and cement) are plentiful. Other minerals of commercial value to Jordan are manganese and oil shale, a rock from which oil is extracted by distillation.

The export of phosphate contributes a great deal to the economy, accounting for over 20 percent of export sales. The rock is used in various chemical and industrial processes. The government-owned Jordan

Independent Picture Service

At Al-Jafr, Bedouin have settled into permanent farming communities and now lead lives quite different from their former nomadic ways.

Conveyor belts load phosphate on ships at the Red Sea port of Aqaba. By installing new facilities, Jordanian authorities have greatly increased shipping traffic in the port.

Phosphate Mines Company operates mines at Ruseifa near Amman and at Al-Hasa and Wadi al-Abyad in the south. A new site at Shidiya in the southeast could start production by the late 1980s. A plant on the Dead Sea run by the Arab Potash Company extracts potash from the water by solar evaporation.

Industry

Jordanian manufacturing, which has emerged rapidly, covers a variety of activities. Oil-fueled generators produce ample electricity to power industrial plants. The most important industry processes potash and other minerals, which are sent to a large chemical fertilizer plant south of Aqaba, to an oil refinery at Zarqa, and to a cement plant near Amman. Some of the crude oil refined at Zarqa comes from Saudi Arabia via the Trans-Arabian Pipeline, which cuts across the northern desert region.

Local materials are used to produce consumer goods, such as canned fruits and vegetables, pure olive oil, vegetable fats, batteries, clothing, and other everyday

As part of a mineral exploration program, technicians search for subsoil minerals with electronic equipment. Jordan also continues to search for oil, and testing rigs have tapped small quantities in several regions of the country.

items. Cement, paper, and pharmaceutical factories, plus several marble works, employ thousands of Jordanians. A tannery, some foundries (where metal is cast), and a phosphate plant have day and night shifts. Other full-time industrial activities include milling, oil pressing, bottling and brewing, footwear and furniture manufacturing, glass printing, and canning of cashew nuts and almonds.

Transportation and Communications

Most inland freight in Jordan is transported by road. Jordan has an overland network covering about 3,100 miles, of which 1,500 miles are paved. Local authorities are responsible for road repair. The system connects major cities and towns as well as nearby countries. Syria is linked to Jordan via Ramtha, Jerash, and Amman. From the town of Maan, the Desert Highway links the nation with Saudi Arabia. Jordanians can reach the West Bank by a main highway from Amman to Jericho over the Allenby Bridge.

The Gulf of Aqaba is easily reached from Amman by a fairly new highway, which is the principal route to the sea. All of Jordan's maritime commerce is done through Aqaba. The expanding economy has enabled Jordanians to develop the port city, which handles several million tons of cargo annually.

Major airlines from all parts of the world fly into Jordan. The national airline is the Royal Jordanian Airline (Alia), whose routes span most Arab lands and include stops in London and on the African and European continents several times each week. Since the early 1960s, air transport has become very active, with the main airport in Amman receiving all international carriers.

A road-building crew works to extend a new transportation route across the desert.

Jerash, a city that features both ancient architecture and modern highways, has been a destination for merchants and travelers since the time of the Roman Empire.

The Hashemite Broadcasting Service, established in 1964, is financially independent, though it is responsible to the Ministry of Culture and Information. Broadcasts in Arabic play 20 hours a day and those in English are transmitted 4 hours a day. Jordanian television is received in Israel, Syria, southern Lebanon, and parts of Saudi Arabia. Because most Jordanians are concentrated in a small area of the country, a high percentage of the population can view television broadcasts.

The press enjoys some freedom in Jordan. Four daily newspapers and five weeklies are published. Many magazines, both

Freighters from all over the world berth at Aqaba, bringing needed supplies to Jordan.

monthly and quarterly, are published by governmental and nongovernmental agencies. Some of these publications are issued under private control.

Trade

Jordan's imports have generally exceeded its exports in value. Part of the debt has been made up by taxes sent home from Jordanians working in nearby oil-rich countries and by loans from foreign governments, including Arab neighbors, the United States, and Great Britain. Principal imports by value are mineral fuels—especially crude petroleum—machinery, cereals, iron and steel, and motor vehicles. These products have come mostly from Saudi Arabia, the United States, Japan, Great Britain, West Germany, and Italy.

Cement, stone for construction, phosphate fertilizer, clothing, fruits and vegetables, pharmaceuticals, and wood products are leading exports. They go mostly to Iraq, Saudi Arabia, India, Romania, Pakistan, and Kuwait.

Courtesy of United Nations

Merchandise is unloaded from a steamer to a lighter, or barge, at the port of Aqaba. One of the most modern ports in the Middle East, Aqaba handles heavy shipping traffic.

Courtesy of United Nations

The mineral explorations program in Amman seeks to increase the export of mineral products in order to improve the Jordanian economy.

Visitors to Jordan tour the country on camels, following caravan trails established by the Romans.

Tourism

Though the loss of the West Bank—with its historical and religious towns, such as Jerusalem, Bethlehem, Nablus, and Jericho—was a severe blow to Jordanian tourism, the nation is now devoting much effort to encourage the industry. The Ministry of Tourism and Antiquities promotes the East Bank as an alternative Holy Land, and steps have been taken to

Tourists *(above)* in Amman walk along walls built by the Romans. Among other sites in Amman are a Roman reservoir and a Byzantine church. Ruins of a desert castle *(right),* one of several eighth-century Umayyad palaces, are among Jordan's little-known attractions. Luxurious rest houses, the castles contained spacious living quarters for the Muslim caliphs and their families, as well as rooms for servants and horses.

One way to reach the hidden city of Petra is on horseback, accompanied by a Jordanian guide.

Photo by Andrew E. Beswick

Courtesy of Jordan Information Bureau, Washington, D.C.

The sunny beaches and warm waters of the Red Sea at Aqaba attract Jordanians as well as foreigners on vacation.

preserve historical sites—such as Jerash, Petra, and Wadi Rumm—and to build better roads and resort facilities.

About one million foreign visitors spent over $500 million in Jordan in the early 1980s. Tourist festivals are advertised extensively with huge, inviting posters. The events include the Camel and Horse Festival, the Water-Ski Festival, the Jordanian Theater Festival, and the Roman amphitheater performances put on by both local and foreign groups each year.

Little-known attractions of Jordan include the desert castles in the eastern part of the country, most of which were used by the Umayyad caliphs around the eighth century A.D. The caliphs' main residence was in Damascus, but they enjoyed life in the desert and would move with their attendants back to the land where their Bedouin ancestors originated.

The Future

Although the pressures that exist around and within Jordan are serious, the nation has remained relatively peaceful despite its Middle Eastern location. War against Israel and the subsequent influx of thousands of Palestinians into Jordan have created social and economic hardships. Jordan has handled these disruptions by absorbing refugees and by making efforts to normalize the lives of its citizens.

Jordan's future, however, is related to its king and his ability to satisfy the different peoples within his country as well as the leaders of neighboring countries. Even though Jordan has made considerable advances in the areas of economic and social welfare, it is still a developing nation with much to improve. Nevertheless, Jordanians are hopeful that their country will eventually overcome its problems and will flourish.

Recent studies indicate that children make up over half of Jordan's population. Young people, therefore, represent a valuable resource for the nation's future.

Index